ROCKS AND MINERALS

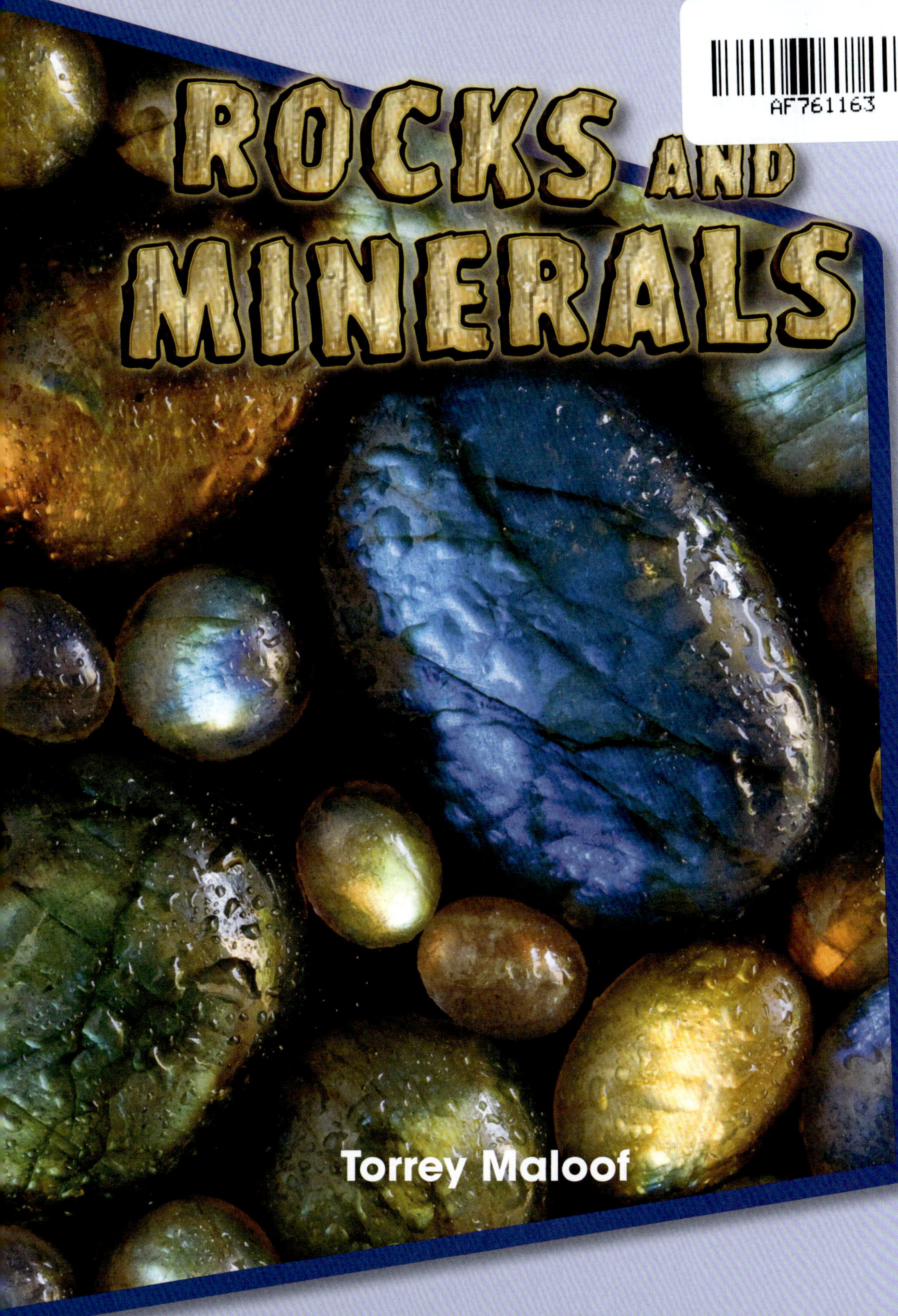

Torrey Maloof

Consultants

Sally Creel, Ed.D.
Curriculum Consultant

Leann Iacuone, M.A.T., NBCT, ATC
Riverside Unified School District

Image Credits: p.25 (top) Mc Donald Wildlife Ph / age fotostock; p.23 (top) Manus Hüller/dieKleinert/Alamy; p.22–23 NASA; pp.28–29 (illustrations) J.J. Rudisill; all other images from Shutterstock.

Library of Congress Cataloging-in-Publication Data

Maloof, Torrey, author.
Rocks and minerals / Torrey Maloof ; consultant, Sally Creel, Ed.D., curriculum consultant, Leann Iacuone, M.A.T., NBCT, ATC Riverside Unified School District, Jill Tobin, California Teacher of the Year semi-finalist Burbank Unified School District.
pages cm
Summary: "Earth is made up of different types of rock. There are three main types of rocks: igneous, sedimentary, and metamorphic. You have probably seen all of these different rocks—you just didn't know it!" — Provided by publisher.
Audience: K to grade 3.
Includes index.
ISBN 978-1-4807-4610-7 (pbk.)
ISBN 978-1-4807-5077-7 (ebook)
1. Rocks—Juvenile literature.
2. Minerals—Juvenile literature.
3. Petrology—Juvenile literature. I. Title.
QE432.2.M25 2015
552—dc23

2014014119

Teacher Created Materials
5301 Oceanus Drive
Huntington Beach, CA 92649-1030
http://www.tcmpub.com

ISBN 978-1-4807-4610-7

Table of Contents

Almost Anywhere 4

Rock Types 6

The Rock Cycle. 20

Rocking Resources 24

Let's Do Science! 28

Glossary. 30

Index 31

Your Turn! 32

Almost Anywhere

Look up, down, and all around! Almost anywhere you look, there are rocks. Earth itself is made of rock. There are even rocks in outer space. Mountains and beaches are made of rocks. Buildings and roads can be made of rocks, too.

Meteorites are rocks that have fallen to the ground from outer space.

There are rocks that are young and rocks that are ancient. Some rocks are enormous, and some rocks are tiny. Certain rocks are tough and strong, while others are soft and delicate. Rocks can be really rough or really smooth. Rocks come in various shapes and colors. But all rocks have interesting stories to tell.

Crazy About Rocks

Some scientists study rocks. They love to learn about them. These scientists are called *geologists*.

Rock Types

Have you ever baked a cake? To bake a cake, you need ingredients. You use things such as flour, sugar, and salt. Then, you mix them all together. The ingredients that make rocks are called **minerals**. Almost all rocks are made of minerals. Minerals are substances that are formed underground. Most rocks are made of two or more minerals.

Cool Crystals

Each mineral has its own shape. These special shapes are called *crystals*.

There are three main types of rocks. Each type forms in a different way.

Igneous Rocks

One type of rock is **igneous** (IG-nee-uhs) rock. The word *igneous* means "from fire." This is the perfect word to describe this type of rock. Igneous rocks form deep inside Earth. There, it's very hot. In fact, it's so hot that the rocks are liquid! This liquid rock is called **magma**.

Mineral Makeup

Quartz and feldspar (FELD-spahr) are two types of minerals. They are found in granite.

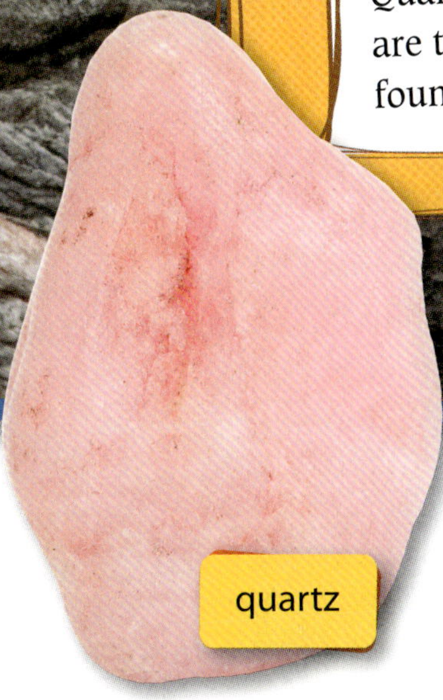

Slowly, the magma cools. Then, it turns into solid igneous rock. Granite is a common type of igneous rock. Sometimes, the magma cools underground. But other times, it makes it all the way to Earth's surface. When this happens, it makes for quite a volcanic eruption!

There are openings in Earth's surface called **volcanoes**. Sometimes, the magma gets really hot underground. It will not cool. Instead, it keeps moving up toward Earth's surface. Then, it breaks free! It shoots out of a volcano with great force. The magma is now **lava**. Then it cools fast. It becomes igneous rock.

Pumice is one type of igneous rock that is formed this way. It is very light in weight. It has a lot of gas bubbles in it. Because of this, pumice floats in water!

pumice

Pumice is the lightest rock on Earth. Many people use pumice stones to scrub away dead skin.

Sedimentary Rocks

Over time, rocks break apart into smaller pieces. Water can wear away rocks as it runs over them. Wind can grind away rocks as it blows past them. And ice can cause rocks to splinter and crack. These small pieces of rock are called **sediment**.

Water and wind help move the sediment. They push the sediment into oceans and lakes. There, it piles up in layers. The top layers get heavy. They push on the bottom layers until they turn to solid rock. This is one way **sedimentary** rocks are formed.

A stream slowly wears away at rocks.

Sandstone is worn away by wind.

Finding Fossils

Fossils can be found in some sedimentary rocks. They are made from the bones or shells of living things.

The **remains** of plants and animals can also make rocks. If a shellfish dies, its shell falls to the ocean floor. Over time, a lot of shells pile up. The pressure builds. This forms sedimentary rocks. Limestone is formed this way.

Rock salt is a type of sedimentary rock. It is formed when water runs over rocks. The minerals in the rocks become part of the water. Then, the water **evaporates**. It leaves rock salt behind. This mostly occurs in caves.

rock salt

Metamorphic Rocks

Earth has several layers. The inner core in the very center of Earth is solid. It's incredibly hot! Next is an outer, liquid core. Then, there is a layer called the *mantle*. It is made of liquid rock. The last layer is called the *crust*. It is in the crust that **metamorphic** rocks are formed.

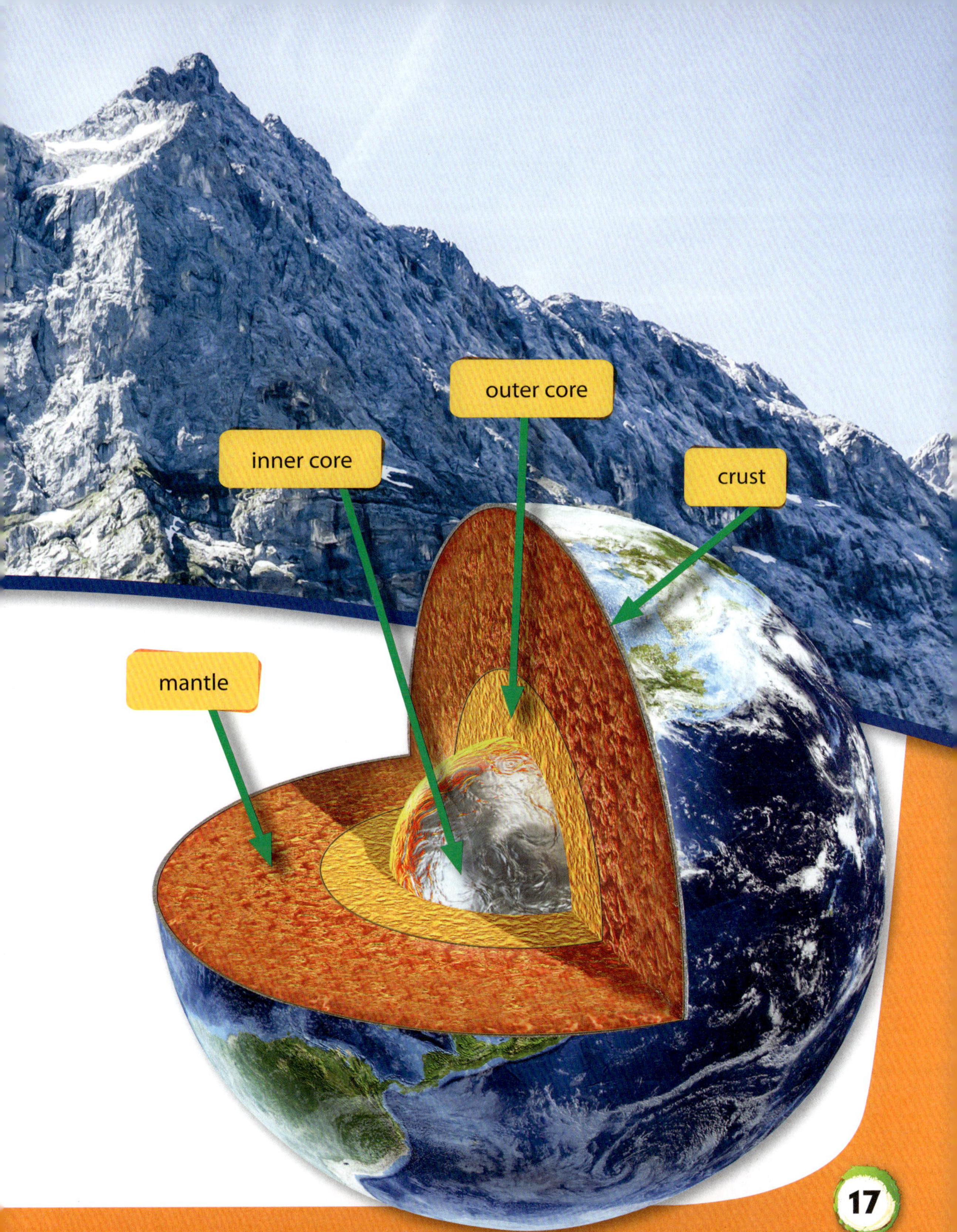
outer core
inner core
crust
mantle

Metamorphic rocks are made deep in Earth's crust. There, the pressure builds. It is also very hot. The heat and pressure work together. They twist and bend the rocks. The minerals in the rocks change. This turns the rock into metamorphic rock.

For example, shale is a sedimentary rock. But when heat and pressure are added, it changes. It turns into slate. If even more pressure is added, it will change again! It turns into schist.

Limestone is a sedimentary rock, too. When heat and pressure are added to limestone, it changes into marble.

Marble Man

There is a famous statue of President Abraham Lincoln in Washington, DC. The statue is carved from marble.

The Rock Cycle

Some things happen over and over in the same order. This is called a *cycle*. A rock can transform over millions of years. It can change from one type of rock to another. This is called the *rock cycle*.

The cycle can start with igneous rock. This type of rock is formed when hot magma cools. Then, wind and water break apart the rock. Tiny pieces of the rock are carried away by wind and water. This sediment travels to oceans and lakes.

The water slowly breaks apart these rocks.

Rock Cycle

The chart below shows how rocks continuously change in the rock cycle.

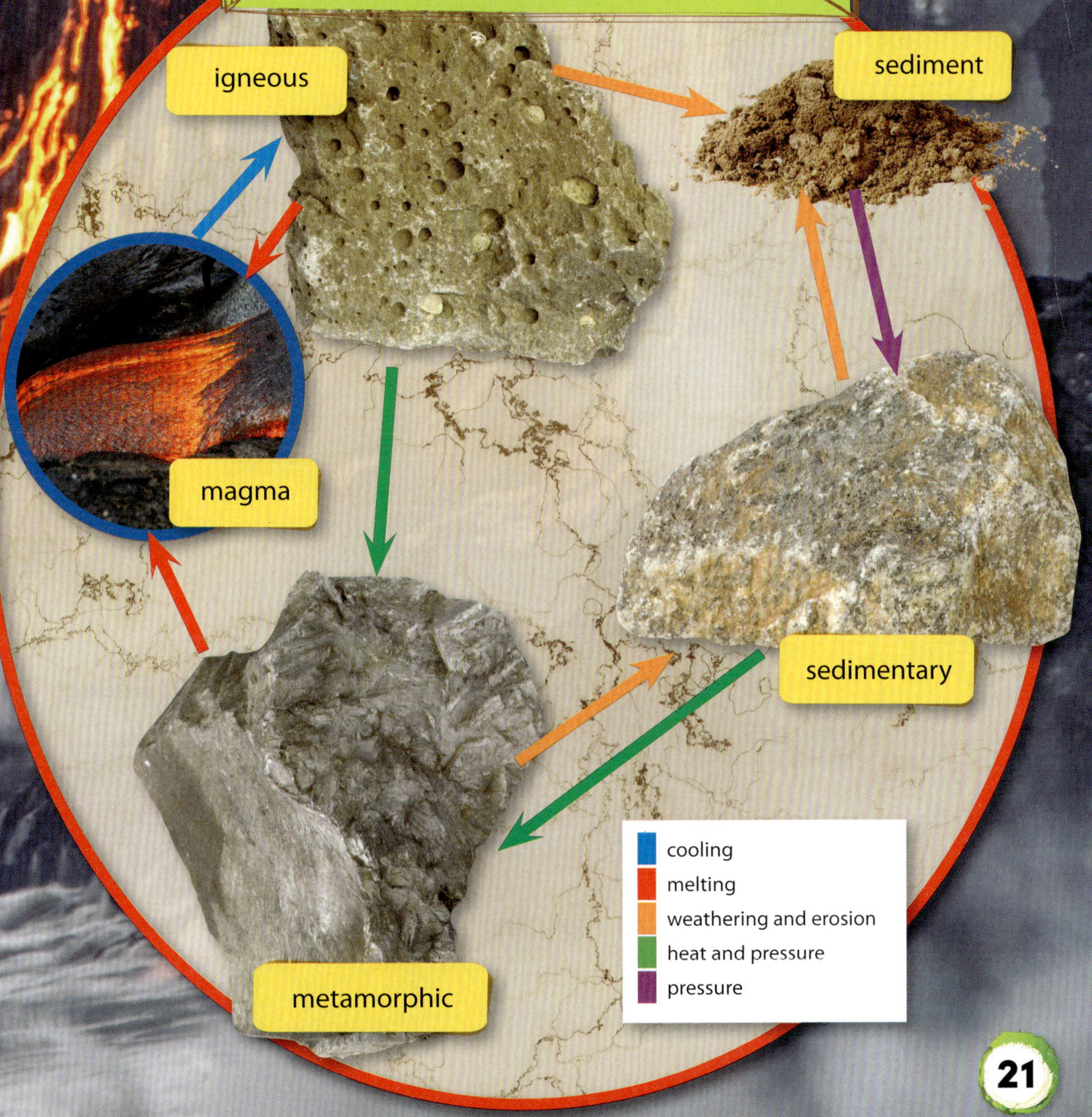

When sediment reaches oceans and lakes, it settles on the floor. Layers of rock pile up over time. Pressure builds. Over many years, a new kind of rock is formed. It is now sedimentary rock.

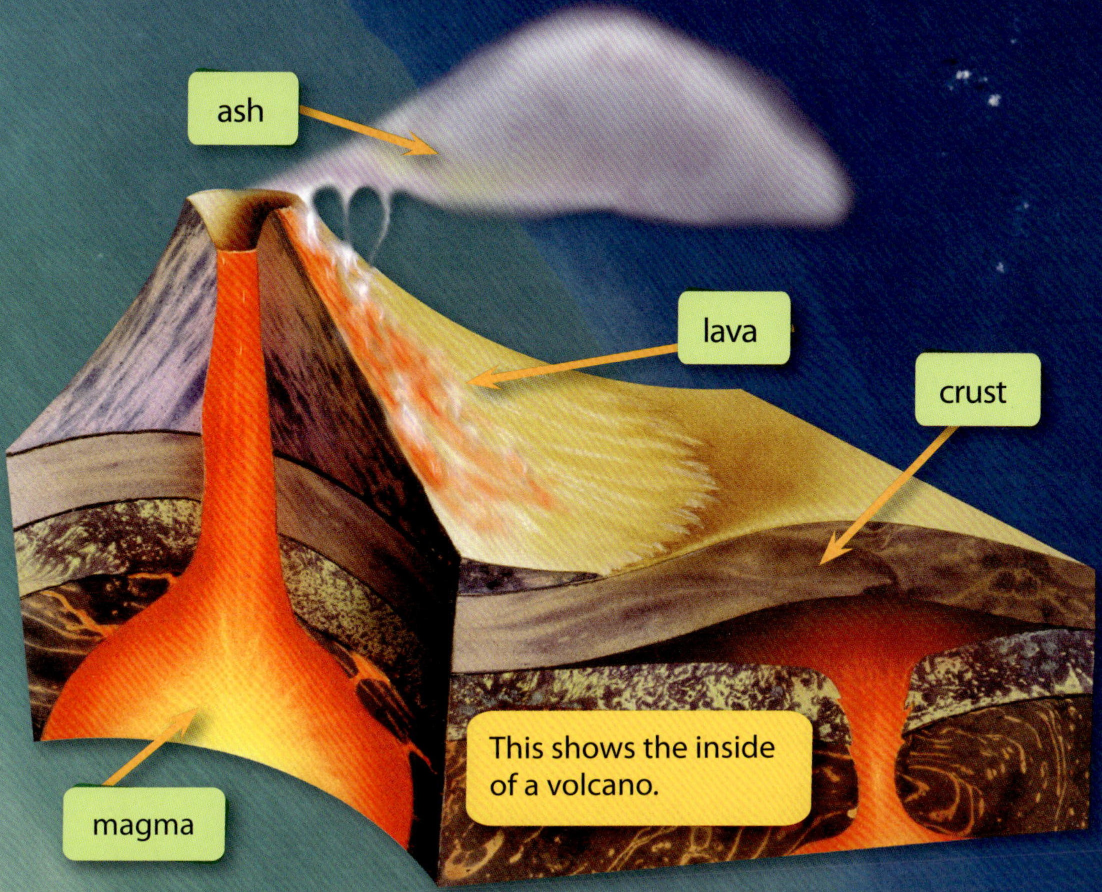

Over time, more pressure and heat build up. The rock starts to change once more. It turns into metamorphic rock. Next, Earth's crust pushes the rock deep into the mantle. There, the rock melts and turns into magma. The magma is then pushed toward Earth's crust. When it cools, it forms igneous rock. The cycle starts again!

Rocking Resources

Rocks have helped people for thousands of years. Long ago, people used rocks as tools and weapons. Rocks helped early humans hunt. They used rocks to dig in the ground, make art, and build grand structures.

Stonehenge is a large circle of giant rocks made by people long ago.

People long ago made tools, such as arrowheads, out of rocks.

Rocks are **natural resources**. These are things that occur in nature. People use these resources to make other things. Many of the metals people use come from the minerals in rocks. Iron and coal come from rocks. Iron is used to make steel. Coal is used to make fuel. It would be hard to go one day without rocks and minerals.

Animals Rock!

Rocks help animals, too! Monkeys and sea otters use rocks as tools. They use rocks to crack open nuts and shells to eat.

Rocks and minerals are important. But they are also beautiful. Some of the most famous landmarks in the world are made from rocks. The Taj Mahal is made from marble. Mount Rushmore is made from granite. The pyramids in Egypt are made from limestone.

A Stunning Surprise

Geodes look dull on the outside. But inside, they are lovely. Geodes are rocks that are hollow and lined with rich crystals.

outside of a geode

inside of a geode

There are even rocks that are out of this world! The moon is made of igneous rock. Asteroids and meteoroids are rocks that fly through space. Rocks and minerals are all around. They help us live. And they help us understand our world.

Taj Mahal

Gold is a metal that is sometimes found in rocks. People search for it because it is worth a lot of money.

Let's Do Science!

Most rocks are made from minerals. Sometimes the minerals form crystals. See for yourself!

What to Get

- 2 measuring spoons
- 2 plastic cups filled halfway with hot water
- magnifying glass
- marker
- table salt and Epsom salts

What to Do

1. Use the marker to label one cup *table salt* and the other cup *Epsom salts*.

2. Use a measuring spoon to add 5 teaspoons of salt into the cup labeled *table salt*. Use the other measuring spoon to add 5 teaspoons of Epsom salts into the other cup.

3. Place both cups in a safe place. Let the water evaporate. It will take about one week.

4. When the water has completely evaporated, look at the bottom of the cup. Use the magnifying glass to study what you see.

Glossary

evaporates—changes from a liquid to a gas

igneous—a type of rock formed when a hot liquid rock cools

lava—hot, liquid rock above Earth's surface

magma—hot, liquid rock below Earth's surface

metamorphic—a type of rock that has changed form under great heat and pressure

minerals—substances that are formed underground

natural resources—things found in nature that can be used to make other things

remains—the parts or body of a dead person, plant, or animal

sediment—very small pieces of rock, such as sand, gravel, and dust

sedimentary—a type of rock made from small pieces of rock, such as sand, gravel, and dust

volcanoes—mountains with holes in the tops or sides that sometimes send out rocks, ash, and lava in a sudden explosion

Index

coal, 25

granite, 8–9, 26

igneous rock, 8–10, 27

iron, 25

limestone, 15, 18, 26

magma, 8–10, 20–23

marble, 18–19, 26

metamorphic rock, 16, 18, 21, 23

natural resources, 25

pumice, 10–11

salt, 6, 15, 28–29

schist, 18

sedimentary rock, 12, 14–15, 18, 21–22

shale, 18

slate, 18

Your Turn!

Rock Walk

Take a walk around your block with an adult. Keep your eyes open for anything that is made from rocks or minerals. Write a list of all the items you find. Are there any items in your home or school that are made from rocks or minerals? List those, too!